GW01606789

Marc Déceneux
Doctor of History of Art
Lecturer on Historical Monuments
at the Abbey of Mont Saint Michel

Mont Saint Michel

« Then a battle started in Heaven :
Michael and his angels fought the dragon.
The dragon fought and so did his angels,
but they did not win and they no longer had a place in Heaven.
Then he fell, the great dragon, the ancient serpent,
he who is called Devil and Satan...
And he landed on the sand by the sea...

Then one of the seven angels came..
And he carried me in the spirit to a great high mountain
and showed me the Holy City, Jerusalem,
which came down from Heaven beside God, possessing the glory of God... »

(*Extracts from* the Book of Revelations)

Photographs : Luigi Levak

ÉDITIONS OUEST-FRANCE
13, rue du Breil, Rennes

A natural marvel

To the left :
the Mont seen from the south-west at low tide

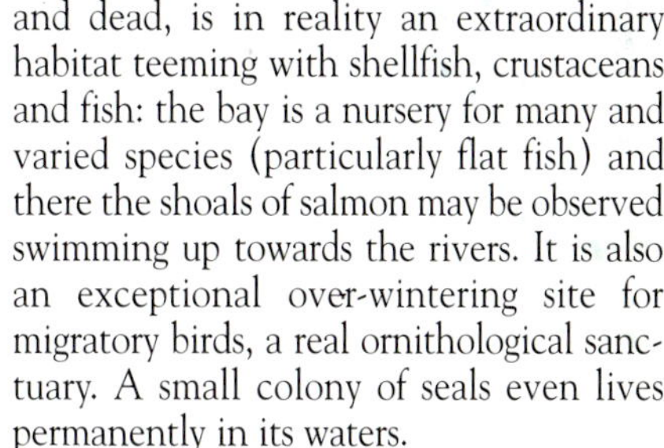

The rock of Mont Saint Michel, like that of Tombelaine, three kilometres to the north and Mont Dol, 23 kilometres to the west, is a vestige of the mountains formed by the upheavals of the Hercynian era, 600 million years ago. The bay which surrounds it, an expanse of 45,000 hectares, is the arena for one of the strongest tides in the world. When the influence of the sun and the moon coincide, a spring tide is caused which at the equinoxes can reach a height of 15 metres. At such times the tide goes out some 18 kilometres, then rushes back to cover the sand-flats, advancing at a speed of 62 metres per minute, or one metre per second!

This vast expanse of "tangue" - a mixture of sand and mud - which appears empty and dead, is in reality an extraordinary habitat teeming with shellfish, crustaceans and fish: the bay is a nursery for many and varied species (particularly flat fish) and there the shoals of salmon may be observed swimming up towards the rivers. It is also an exceptional over-wintering site for migratory birds, a real ornithological sanctuary. A small colony of seals even lives permanently in its waters.

But this unique site is in danger. Since the 11th century man has been attempting, through the creation of dykes, to transform the foreshore into fertile agricultural land. This venture has been continuing, but with far more effective methods, since 1856: thanks to new dykes, to the canalization of the Couesnon and also to the expertise of Dutch engineers, more than 4,000 hectares of the foreshore have been reclaimed into polders.

This drying-out of the bay is furthered even more by the natural phenomenon of silting-up. As each tide goes out, the sea leaves behind a deposit of "tangue" of which the level is rising constantly. Little by little, specific vegetation (spartina and saltwort) is colonizing the shoreline, soon taken over by the plants which make up the "herbu" (the salt marshes). The land is thus fixed and stabilizes for good.

Up to the last century, this phenomenon was counteracted by the effect of the flow of water from the rivers which ran into the bay, which pushed back the sediment as it was deposited. But these water courses (Couesnon, Sélune, Sée and Guintre), are now canalized, re-routed and weakened and so do not fulfil their cleansing function and the salt marshes are progressing more and more quickly, encircling the Mont like a giant pair of pincers.

Since the 1970s, research has been taking place which should bring about, after some extensive work in the next few years, a stabilization of the silting-up and so the preservation of the island quality which gives the rock all its historical and spiritual meaning.

Below :
a wonderful, friendly encounter: one of the seals of the bay.
Photo André Mauxion

The origins - The myths and the legends

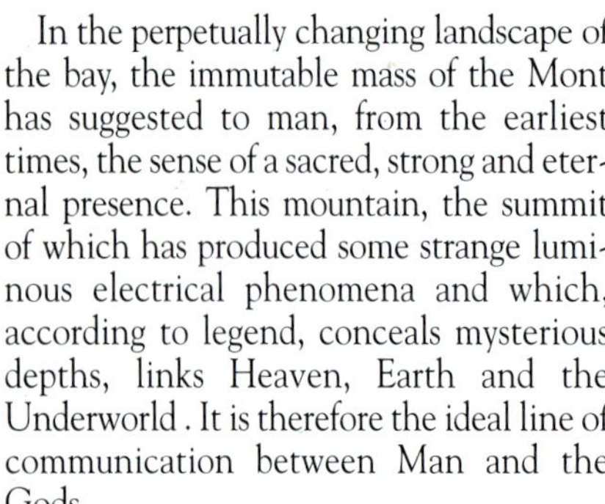

In the perpetually changing landscape of the bay, the immutable mass of the Mont has suggested to man, from the earliest times, the sense of a sacred, strong and eternal presence. This mountain, the summit of which has produced some strange luminous electrical phenomena and which, according to legend, conceals mysterious depths, links Heaven, Earth and the Underworld . It is therefore the ideal line of communication between Man and the Gods.

Since the Neolithic period, between 5 BC and 3 BC, the rock has been a sacred place. Various pieces of corroborative evidence indicate that during this period there was a megalithic funerary monument (a dolmen or passage grave) near the summit. The Mont is also linked with the menhirs on the surrounding hills, which are in perfect alignment with it in a line continuing for about thirty kilometres.

The traditional legends associated with these megaliths are all linked, one way or another, with Mont Saint Michel. They give a glimpse of the emergence of prehistoric mythological themes, since preserved in the fertile material of folklore. At the heart of this vanished mythology, the confrontation between two giants can be linked with the fundamental myths of the oldest religions: two generations oppose each other; the older, which symbolizes the chaos and disorder of the beginning, is deposed from power by his successor whose heavenly and organizing nature will ensure the regulation of the great natural and cosmic cycles. The peaceful Neolithic farmers thus saw, in the bay, the special place in which in a mythical past, the destiny of the world was decided.

Nearer to our own era, the Celts also left a deep impression on local legend. Like Ireland and Wales, our region is haunted by stories of marine cataclysms and floods: under the sands of the bay there are drowned towns and forests... Later the Benedictines collected these legends for their chronicles and, moving them through time, turned them into the fable of the Forest of Scissy, carried away by an apocalyptic tidal wave linked to the apparition of the Archangel.

In this context of the Celtic myths, the story of Mont Saint Michel is closely associated with that of Mont Dol. The former was known in the Gallo-Roman period as the Gate of Hercules. The name of this Roman divinity is a transposition of the Gaulish god Ogmios, an important figure in the Celtic pantheon. A sovereign and warlike divinity, Ogmios is the god of eloquence and magic writing; he conducted the company of the dead to the Other World and one offers one's enemies to him so that he may bind them with his spell and render them impotent.

In Celtic mythology, Ogmios is in rivalry with his brother Taranis, the Gaulish Jupiter, to whom Mont Dol was dedicated,

Mont Dol seen from the terrace of the abbey church at Mont Saint Michel : the church is on the same axis as the line which links the two mountains

Photo Marc Déceneux

known at that time as Mont de Jupiter. Unlike Ogmios, Taranis is a peaceful and benevolent god, who reigns over the sky, controlling the weather and watching over friendship and the observance of agreements.

The legends of the bay, romanticized in the 12th century, retain a memory of the strife-torn relationship which these two divinities, under other names, have fought out. They also enable us to understand why, in the 6th century, the great Gaulish missionary St. Samson dedicated a chapel on Mont Dol to St. Michael. The Gauls thought that Taranis had once vanquished a monster which was half-giant and half-serpent and which was threatening the safety of the world: the dedication of Mont Dol to the Archangel who conquered the diabolical dragon was thus keeping alive a familiar image.

The mythical link between the two mountains is reflected in the local legends: they recount that the battle between the Archangel and the Devil began on Mont Dol and finished on Mont Saint Michel, from where the Archangel flew away with a beat of his wings when his adversary was hurled into the waves. Perhaps we have there the memory of the transfer, during the Merovingian period, of the cult of St. Michael from one mountain to the other.

he island of ombelaine, seen rom the east, gives n idea of the Mont efore any building ook place.

Iont Saint Michel een from Iont Dol.

The foundation and the early centuries

The origins of the Christian cult at Mont Saint Michel are only known to us through monastic texts which weave history, legend and mystical speculation closely together. This religious literature gives glimpses, in the mists of the High Middle Ages, of the presence of hermits on the rock. These solitary people had links with a monastery close by on the mainland, which supported them.

In 708, Aubert, the Bishop of Avranches, - honoured, according to the chronicles, by a vision of St. Michael - decided to create a shrine dedicated to the Archangel on Mont Tombe. This initiative could have been for several reasons. In the political context of the period, promotion of the cult of the Archangel was a gesture of allegiance to the Mayor of the Palais, Pepin de Herstal, sword-bearer to King Childebert III just as St.Michael is to God. This cult, on the other hand, was very popular at the time: the neighbouring diocese of Dol had dedicated the rock of Mont Dol to him. The foundation by St. Aubert can thus be considered as having been a manifestation of the competition between two bishoprics.

The oldest texts which tell us of the foundation give a brief description of the shrine built at the beginning of the 8th century. Built with blocks of rough granite, crudely superposed, it had a circular design and was situated near the summit of the rock on the western side with a floor area large enough to hold about one hundred people. The unusual design and form of this first chapel are a reminder of the grotto of Monte Gargano, in the Apulian mountains of Southern Italy: St. Michael appeared in this cavern at the end of the 5th century; and it is from then that the cult of the Archangel began to spread over the Western World. Thus from the very beginning the new shrine belonged to a prestigious movement. Of Aubert's oratory there remains today the far wall which was found in 1960 behind the Carolingian masonry in the apse of Notre Dame sous Terre: an opening enables visitors to contemplate this moving relic.

Bishop Aubert, in order to ensure the formalities of the cult were observed, founded a college of twelve monks and endowed it with the income from the episcopal lands around Avranches. All that is known of this first community is the criticism written of them by their Benedictine successors. It is possible to imagine that it was organized in the manner of the old Celtic monasteries and that the monks lived under a severe regime, similar to that of St. Columbanus, which combined collective worship, the interminable recitation of psalms and a solitary seclusion which was almost hermitic, punctuated by harsh mortifications. The testimony of a pilgrim from the end of the 9th century tells us that, in addition, the Abbot in charge was a Breton.

The success of Mont Saint Michel as a site of pilgrimage was established very quickly and the construction of new buildings became essential. A fairly large church was built on the summit (its foun-

Opposite, top : ***the chapel of Saint Aubert (15th century) is, according to legend, built on a rock which fell miraculously from the summit during construction of the first shrine.***

Opposite, bottom : ***the ancient pre-Romanesque chapel of Notre Dame sous Terre.***

The skull of Saint Aubert

A legend, first related around A.D. 1000 by the Benedictines, tells how the Archangel, appalled by the unbelief of Bishop Aubert on the occasion of his third appearance to him, perforated his skull by touching him with his finger of light. The head of Saint Aubert, for centuries an object of veneration for pilgrims, escaped damage during the French Revolution. It is today kept at Avranches in the treasury of the Church of Saint Gervais. This mysterious relic is, in reality, a trepanned skull, certainly prehistoric, which was discovered on the rock by the monks when they arrived there, during their construction work. It is proof that in very ancient times, the Mont was already a holy place used as a burial site.

dations were found during excavations of the current Abbey) and below and to the west, a solidly built chapel replaced Aubert's modest oratory. This lower shrine has been preserved: it is the Chapel of Notre Dame sous Terre (Our Lady Under Ground), which huddles under the terrace of the Church.

This Chapel probably built between 900 and 930, bears all the hallmarks of Carolingian architecture, which developed from Roman methods of construction: very thick masonry made of ashlar stone set in a bed of mortar, bare walls with no attempt at pattern, arches made of flat bricks. It has two parallel naves, each ending in a small vaulted choir: this highly unusual double structure was inspired by that of the Chapel of St. Michael at Mont Dol. Notre Dame sous Terre is also built on the road linking Mont Saint Michel to Mont Dol. All of this bears witness to the close relationship between the Mont and Brittany which existed in the Middle Ages.

The monastic period

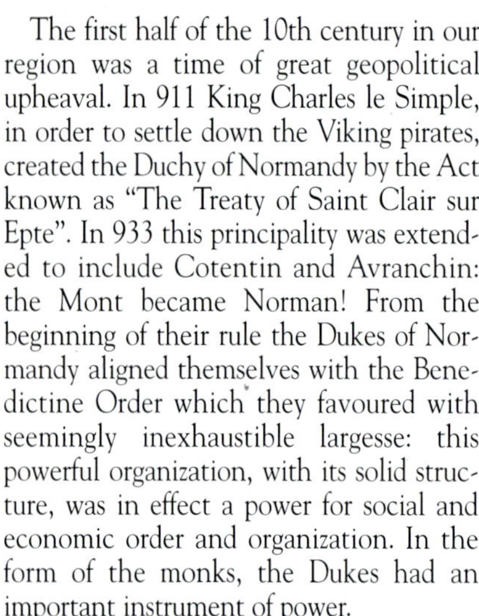

The first half of the 10th century in our region was a time of great geopolitical upheaval. In 911 King Charles le Simple, in order to settle down the Viking pirates, created the Duchy of Normandy by the Act known as "The Treaty of Saint Clair sur Epte". In 933 this principality was extended to include Cotentin and Avranchin: the Mont became Norman! From the beginning of their rule the Dukes of Normandy aligned themselves with the Benedictine Order which they favoured with seemingly inexhaustible largesse: this powerful organization, with its solid structure, was in effect a power for social and economic order and organization. In the form of the monks, the Dukes had an important instrument of power.

Mont Saint Michel, on the frontier with Brittany, was both a strategically sensitive point and an important political symbol. In addition, in 966, Duke Richard I had driven the monks off the rock, suspecting them of being sympathetic to Brittany, and replaced them with Benedictines from the great Norman Abbey of St. Wandrille, near Rouen. It was then that the Mont began to expand.

The feudal power of the abbey rapidly found expression in the amassing of a considerable fortune in property. Within a few score years, the domain of the monastery extended, thanks to the generosity of the nobles, across the whole of France, and also into Brittany, Italy and even England: St. Michael's Mount, for example, in West Cornwall was a priory for Mont Saint Michel from about 1033 or 1034. This tiny monastery, on the summit of a rock accessible at low tide, was a miniature replica of the famous Norman abbey...

Benedictine thought was also expressed in the liturgical pomp, revealed to us by the manuscripts in the library. They describe with precision the processions and ceremonies which marked the days and years of the regular calendar, and the chants, the ornaments and the precious objects used in the services. The masses, celebrated with beauty and grandeur, represented for the

The earliest representation of the Mont (the Bayeux Tapestry - end of 11th century).
Photo reproduced with special permission from the Town of Bayeux

A Benedictine monk at prayer in a manuscript from the abbey (Manuscript 213 in Avranches library - early 15th century).
Photo from the Municipal library at Avranches

marvelling pilgrims a prefiguration of the supernatural harmony of the liturgy celebrated by the angels in the New Jerusalem.

In addition, the Benedictine monks, as their motto says, prayed and worked. The monks of the Mont, the elite at the centre of the social elite which the regular clergy considered itself to be, did not lower themselves to manual work. Their work was essentially intellectual. They copied, illuminated, studied and wrote. The catalogue of their prestigious library, the bulk of which, two hundred manuscripts, is now kept in Avranches, bears witness to a wide-ranging curiosity. The scriptorium (the copyists' room) of course produced religious books, but also works on history, science and nature. The works of antiquity are also present, notably Aristotle's treatises, of which Mont Saint Michel was, in the Romanesque period, one of the leading centres of study.

But above all, the monks created a place

by the monks shows that it is a transposition of the great biblical themes.

The history of the foundation by St. Aubert, as rewritten by the monks, is point for point and in every detail a faithful transfer of the account of the revelation to Moses. Mont Saint Michel thus becomes a new Sinai! Noah's Ark and the Temple of Jerusalem are also used as references by the monks, which are often quoted in the chronicles, and were used to calculate the proportions and the structure of the monastery's architecture.

Finally, the miracles, related with some delectation by the scribe monks, were inspired by the most dramatic episodes in the Book of Revelations. The sandy shore becomes, under their pen, the terrible setting for a prophetic vision of the end of time and the rock a prefiguration of the New Jerusalem, where the chosen, after Judgement Day, will bask forever in the divine vision.

St. Michael's Mount in Cornwall, England.
Photo Marc Déceneux

of pilgrimage destined to become one of the most important in the medieval Western World. The success of the undertaking lay in the strength of its image. The Benedictines were also rapidly to create a gilded legend which made the rock into a major site in the religious geography of the Christian world. Analysis of the myth developed

By the year AD 1000, the Mont offered pilgrims this image of the "City of God" which harmoniously gathered together "those who work, those who fight and those who pray". Still today, this historic place gives us the means to understand this perfect microcosm of the medieval imagination.

"Those who work"...

The visitor to Mont Saint Michel, before reaching the monastery which crowns the rock, first encounters the picturesque village which scales its southern flank. In spite of the many changes and reconstructions, inevitable given the constraints of such a restricted urban space, its atmosphere barely differs from that encountered by the pilgrims in the Middle Ages. Let us allow our imaginations to carry us back several centuries.

Once through the great gateway, an amazing world is revealed, noisy and colourful. All along the single narrow street which climbs the steep hill, half-timbered houses jostle each other for space: every one is a souvenir shop. Vendors of pious odds and ends, sellers of pictures and "knick-knacks" shout out to the pilgrims and offer them cheap trash: figures painted on wood, cloth or shells, trumpets made of pottery or bronze and a whole ironmonger's worth of lead and tin. Badges bearing the effigy of the Archangel for attaching to one's clothes or hat, sets of clasps for necklaces and coats, rings inscribed with the motto "Aultre ne Veut" (No Other), phials for collecting holy water from the church or a little sand from the bay - all of this can be found from one shop to another, the length of the street. The souvenirs, originally made on the Mont, soon entered quasi-industrial production and from the 14th century were mass produced in Paris and shipped to Normandy.

The other principal business of the Mont is, of course, hotel-keeping. Taverns and inns, as numerous as the shops, display their painted metal signs over the street, adding to the riot of colour everywhere. These establishments offer the pilgrim, hungry after his walk across the sand-flats, the specialities of local charcuterie and fish from the bay, accompanied by the wine which the abbey buys duty-free and resells to the merchants: thus one may enjoy, for a modest sum, wine from Poitou and Anjou and some excellent Bergerac produced in the vineyards owned by the Abbey in the South West. And one must make sure one doesn't forget the national beverage, as mentioned by one of the old Abbey chroniclers, referring to "brains overheated by the Normandy cider..."

At the end of the 17th century the village consisted, according to a military report, of "some 50 to 60 houses, all taverns, haberdashers or small shops" with a population of 250 souls. Today, the number of permanent inhabitants is only about thirty, but the general atmosphere has not changed. The little shops and the hotel-restaurants are continuing a tradition of welcome nearly thirteen centuries old; the names they bear are those found in the very oldest village records: Le Chapeau Rouge, La Coquille, La Croix Blanche, Le Dauphin, La Licorne, Le Saint Michel, Le Saint Pierre, Le Mouton Blanc, La Sirène, Le Tripot, Le Pot de Cuivre, etc...

Most of the timber houses were replaced at the end of the 19th century, though fol-

Dormer window of La Maison de l'Artichaut and facade of La Maison de la Sirène.

Opposite :
Interior of the parish church.

Mère Poulard

Annette Boutiaut, who was born in 1851, was chambermaid to Madame Corroyer, wife of the architect in charge of the first restoration works. In 1873 she married Victor Poulard, a native of the Mont and opened a restaurant which over the years grew more and more successful, owing to the quality of the service and the local cuisine: it was patronized by the crowned heads of the period and the great names in politics, the arts and the theatre. Annette Poulard retired in 1906 and died in 1931. The simple country omelette which she prepared has today become a spectacular and sophisticated dish, and her name, with its connotations of luxury dining, is used as a brand name on high quality products which are exported all over the world.

lowing the same ground plan. However several of them still survive. One may particularly admire, at the entrance to the village, the house known as " La Maison de l'Arcade" which clings to the ramparts like a limpet, "L'Artichaut" of which the facade, shingled with chestnut-wood, spans the main street, "La Sirène" and "La Typhaine" named after the wife of Bertrand de Guesclin or "La Licorne", which has preserved the stair turrets to its rear. Others, like the Hotel Saint Pierre and the Hotel du Mouton Blanc, are clever modern pastiches, inspired by old dwellings on the Mont shown on a model made at the end of the 17th century.

As if to authenticate the village-like character of the place, situated at the side of the main street is the parish church, dedicated to St. Peter. Built in the 15th and 16th centuries on some old Roman masonry, it houses the silver statue of the Archangel, a place of pilgrimage since 1873. Recent restoration work has brought out the richness of its furnishings and the works of art it conserves.

"Those who fight" : the fortress...

The monastery, heavily fortified at the end of the 14th century by Abbot Pierre le Roy, crowns the rock above the village like a stronghold. This image reminds us that the Abbey was a seignory and the Abbot its seigneur. The gibbet, a potent sign of feudal power, has gone (it was placed to the left of the town gate, on the site of the current bus stop), but the court-room has been preserved: it is the superb "Salle de Bellechaise", above the Abbey entrance and recent restoration work has returned it to its former splendour.

In the medieval world, the first duty of the seigneur was to bear arms for the overlord. The Mont is also a fortress. There is evidence that fortifications have existed since the end of the 10th century, when Duke Richard enclosed with solid walls the Benedictine monastery he had just found ed. However the town was not walled until the second half of the 13th century, doubtless at the instigation of Saint Louis, who made two pilgrimages here.

The first ramparts were greatly increased in size in 1417, while the Hundred Years' War was raging. Abbot Robert Jolivet thus made the Mont impregnable, before himself going over to the English side. The Porte du Roi (King's Gate) also dates from the beginning of the 15th century and closed off the village street with a ditch, a drawbridge, a port cullis and some strong doors in ironclad oak.

After the war, at the end of the reign of Louis XI a new programme of defensive building was begun. The Tour Boucle (1481) also dates from this period, an artillery bastion equipped with low

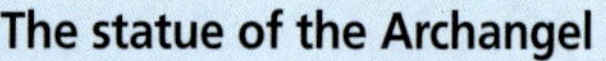

The statue of the Archangel

Some old documents mention, in the 16th century, a gilded statue of the Archangel which stood on top of the bell tower and disappeared in a fire in 1594. However the current statue which tops the spire at a height of 157 metres above sea-level only dates from 1897. The sculptor Emmanuel Frémiet had made the model for it in 1879. It was the architect Victor Petitgrand who decided to have a larger version made by the Monduit workshops who were also responsible for the Statue of Liberty. Four metres high, the statue of the Archangel is made of sheets of embossed copper, bolted onto an iron frame, and it weighs 450 kg. The tips of the sword and the wings act as lightning conductors, which has meant that over the century it has suffered some serious damage. Thus in 1987 it was taken from its place by helicopter, restored, regilded with gold leaf and replaced, once again by air. These operations, very difficult technically, were the subject of enormous media attention at the time.

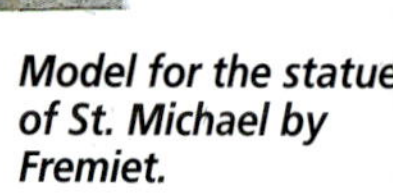

Model for the statue of St. Michael by Fremiet.

Left :
La Porte du Roi (the King's Gate), at the entrance to the Grande Rue.

...and the domain of the seigneur

The spire and the Archangel.

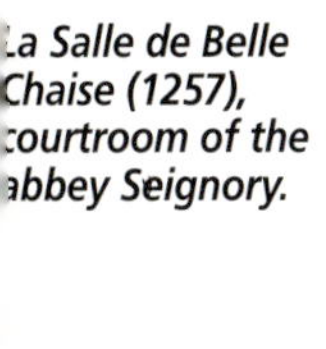

La Salle de Belle Chaise (1257), courtroom of the abbey Seignory.

a Tour Boucle t the end of the 7th century (model nade from the relief nap in Les nvalides).

batteries and with a central conduit which allowed the cannon smoke to clear away. Its pentagonal outline, which gives it a range of fire with no blind spot, was a revolutionary prototype which prefigured standard fortification by more than a century.

The walls were reinforced once more at the beginning of the 16th century. The Tour Gabriel, on the south west of the rock, was built in 1524 and at the same time the entrance defences were also increased: in 1525, one had to pass through three gates to enter the village.

The ramparts which surround the base of Mont Saint Michel thus constitute a genuine anthology of medieval fortification. All this of course had a strong symbolic value, which greatly enhanced the role of the Mont during the Hundred Years' War. In the darkest hours of this period the Mont was practically the only fortified town the English could not take: the sea which surrounded it twice daily made any fixed siege impossible. The legendary garrison of one hundred and nineteen knights and their followers repelled every assault, and after one violent attack in 1433, the enemy was forced to retreat, abandoning its dead and the cannon which can be seen today at the entrance to the village.

Mont Saint Michel then became the symbol of the identity and independence of the Kingdom of France and in 1469 King Louis XI created the military order of the Chevaliers de Saint Michel (Knights of St. Michael) to set seal on the alliance between the Archangel and the French nobility against the enemies of the kingdom.

The mountain was henceforth a rallying point for national feeling. It was to remain so: under the Third Republic, after the Franco-Prussian War, the spirit of revenge (against the Germans this time) overcame secular principles and a statue of the warrior Archangel came to crown the brand new spire of the abbey church!

"Those who pray"...

Above the working village and the feudal walls of the monastery rises the abbey church, just as the clergy once dominated the nobility and the third estate.

Naturally, it is dedicated to the Archangel Michael and its situation on the summit, nearly in Heaven, corresponds perfectly with the cult of this great angelic figure. Michael, of which the Hebrew name Mikael means "He who is like God", is, according to Isaiah, "the Being who surpasses all the other angels in his glory" and he is enthroned in the seventh Heaven, the highest level . He is moreover, in the Book of Revelations, the champion of the celestial armies against the diabolical forces of the Beast. The medieval traditions whim as the conductor of souls in their last voyage to the heavens.

All these attributes make the Archangel the great mediator between the heavenly powers and the terrestrial world. So the shrines dedicated to him are most often established on the highest ground, points of contact between Earth and Heaven. Here are some examples, among the most spectacular: the Rock of Saint Michel d'Aiguilhe at Puy en Velay, Saint Michel de Cuxa in the Pyrenees, the Sagra di San Michele in Piedmont and the wild reef of Skellig Michael in Ireland. The Middle Ages also often saw the consecration of altars to St. Michael in towers or on the upper level of the great church porches, as at Vézelay, Tournus or Saint Benoît sur Loire.

But besides its situation on the summit which was quite usual for a Michaelian shrine, the decision to build the church on the furthermost point of the rock grew out of a highly ambitious mystical concept. The monks, when they developed the gilded legend of the Mont, transposed into the bay the mystery of the biblical mountains: the manuscripts in their library preserve the memory of these pious meditations. The temple perched on the peak of the island seemed to them to be like Noah's Ark placed after the Flood on the top of Mount Ararat. They also compared it to the Temple of Jerusalem on the heights of Mount Zion. The granite peak, scene of strange phenomena of light and the site of divine revelations, evoked for them Mount Sinai, on

The abbey seen from the north-west.

...the abbey, shrine of the heights

which the alliance between God and his people was sealed...

Thus they identified the shrine, suspended in the middle of the sky above the mists which rise from the bay, as the New Jerusalem described in the Book of Revelations, where at the end of time, the chosen will gather together for eternity. These biblical references reveal the aim of the undertaking: through the efforts of the Benedictine monks, Mont Saint Michel was to become a principal feature of the sacred geography of the Christian west!

The implementation of this ambitious project required some technical feats. The tip of the rock has in fact only a tiny area of level ground and it was only possible to build on it the four large pillars of the crossing of the transept, which support the clock tower, and a small section of the nave. The rest of the church, the floor plan of which is in the shape of an immense cross, rests on an artificial platform, made up of four crypts placed at the four points of the compass and which completely encircle the tip of the mountain. These are today to the east the Crypt des Gros Piliers (the Crypt of the Huge Pillars), to the west Notre Dame sous Terre, to the south Saint Martin and to the north Notre Dame des Trente Cierges (Our Lady of the Thirty Candles).

The monastery buildings and the reception rooms were placed below, all around the sides of the rock.. The buildings of the Romanesque monastery covered the western half of the rock and those of the Gothic monastery the eastern half.

This collection of buildings is extremely complex. The various buildings, rebuilt, repaired, extended and altered over the centuries, are criss-crossed by a network of staircases, corridors and passages in the thickness of the walls, which makes them a veritable labyrinth. This is because it was necessary, in a restricted surface area, to reconcile two conflicting requirements: hospitality for the pilgrims, an essential duty according to the Rule, and the enclosure which had to maintain the isolation of the monks.

The Mont seen from the east.

Construction

Right : the north side

1. The abbey church
2. The four crypts
   A : Crypt des Gros Piliers
   (Crypt of the Huge Pillars)
   B : Notre-Dame des Trente Cierges
   (Our Lady of the Thirty Candles)
   C : St. Martin
   D : Notre-Dame-Sous-Terre
   (Our Lady Below Ground)
3. The Romanesque monastery
4. The Gothic monastery
   (La Merveille)

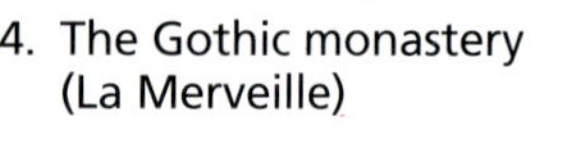

Below : the south side

1. The entrance building :
   Ground floor: Salle des Gardes
   First floor: Courtroom (Belle Chaise)
2. The Abbot's lodgings
3. The terrace of the Saut Gautier
   (Gautier's Leap)
   Below: the Great Wheel
4. The western terrace

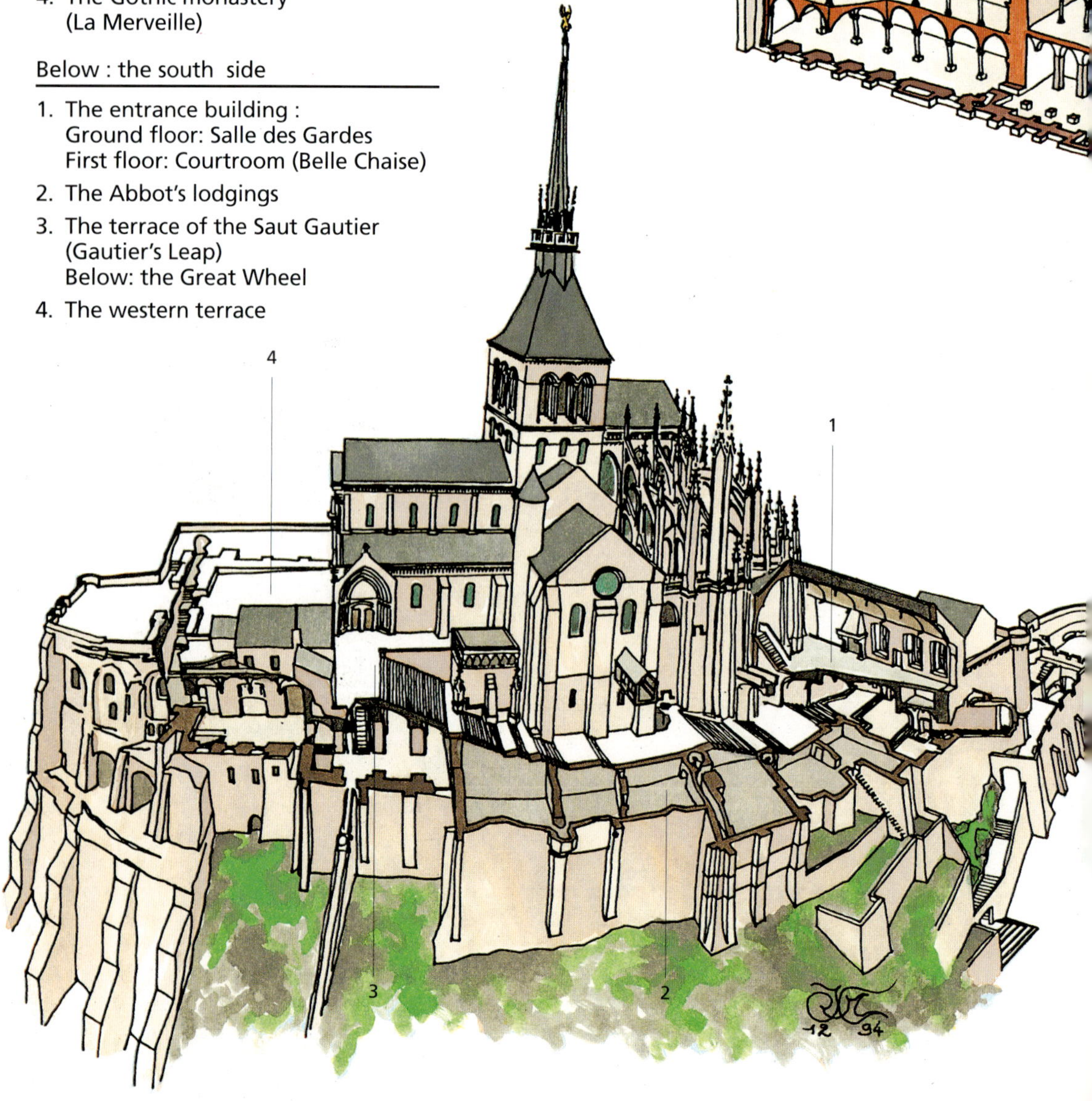

1
4
2
C
A
B
D
3
4
3

The romanesque church

At the same time as they were creating the myth of its foundation, turning the rock into a biblical mountain, the monks were starting the construction of a vast church on the summit, as a fitting place to receive the crowds of pilgrims. Built between 1023 and about 1080, from granite brought by sea from the Iles Chausey, 35 kilometres away, this church has a rich background of symbolism.

The edifice measures 80 metres in length and is at a height of 80 metres above the sand-flats: it therefore fits into a perfect square, a symbol, in medieval times, of the universe created in all its perfection. Its interior rises in a succession of landings, separated by flights of stairs, and from the porch to the choir it rises by five metres in relation to the entrance: this is the structure of the Temple of Solomon in Jerusalem. Finally, the central nave is inscribed inside a rectangle built according to the proportions of Noah's Ark, as stated in the Bible.

The construction of the monument was, for a long time, credited to the Italian Benedictine William de Volpiano, Abbot of Saint Benigne at Dijon and an indefatigable reformer of Norman abbeys. It is now

known that this great monastic figure of the first Millennium had nothing to do

Above : ***Despite having been shortened in the 18th century, the nave has retained its vigorous majesty.***

Left : ***The imposing expanse of the southern arm of the transept..***

Below left : ***The purity of the Romanesque forms of the apse of the Crypt of Saint Martin.***

Below right : ***The intimate space of the Crypt of Notre Dame des Trente Cierges (Our Lady Of the Thirty Candles).***

with the conception of the work. Rather, it should be placed in the context of the great architectural creations of western France and linked with projects in Brittany (Redon c.1010) and especially in Maine (Evron c.980-990).

A large part of the early lower section has been preserved. To the west, the Carolingian chapel of Notre Dame sous Terre lies within Romanesque walls. To the north, the crypt of Notre Dame des Trente Cierges is an intimate and enclosed space; the monks celebrated morning mass there each day and in the evening sang their wonderful Salve Regina, a prelude to the silence of the night. To the south, the crypt of Saint Martin displays the same Romanesque form, but on a more monumental scale: this chapel built outside the monastery walls, which seems to have been used for public gatherings, was probably a funerary crypt for important lay figures, benefactors of the abbey.

The Romanesque choir, which collapsed in 1421, had an apsidial layout and was encircled by an ambulatory, as found in the great pilgrim churches. This type of layout, unknown in Normandy until then, was undoubtedly taken from the prestigious prototype of the Benedictine abbey at Evron. The transept, shortened at the north end in the 13th century, has preserved intact the beautiful Romanesque space of its southern arm. Under the barrel vaulting, of an exceptional height and strength for the period, it is richly decorated (limestone Corinthian capitals, columns framing vast windows, relieving arches enlivening the walls) similar to that of the great narthex at Saint Benoît sur Loire.

The nave, built during the vigorous reign of William the Conqueror, marked a change of style and bore witness to a strong Norman personality. The elevation was on three levels (large archways, triforium, and high windows) as at Jumièges, and the bays, strongly emphasized by linked semi-columns, were detailed by relieving arches under the panelled roof. The volume of the nave was thus arranged in a succession of stages which gave a majestic rhythm to the procession of the faithful towards the altar.

Only a part of this beautiful nave remains today: the north wall, which collapsed in 1103, was rebuilt in a manner more prudent and robust, but less elegant. The original facade, which had an enclosed porch, was replaced in the 12th century by a severe design with two towers, by Abbot Robert de Thorigny, who in 1145 had seen the prototype under construction in Chartres. But these western parts disappeared in 1776, following a fire which necessitated the shortening of the nave: of the seven original bays, three were removed and the western terrace enlarged. Some low walls, put in place during the restoration in 1962, enable the visitor to visualize the missing sections on the modern square in front of the church.

The romanesque monastery

The buildings of the Romanesque monastery, continuously under construction during the 11th and 12th centuries, covered the western half of the rock. At the foot of the walls, on the west face, opened the great archways of the entrance porch. From there, the pilgrims entered the enclosure and reached a monumental staircase - which still remains under the terrace of the church - which took them straight to the square, in front of the great doors of the upper sanctuary.

The monks occupied a long building to the north, which ran along the whole length of the nave of the church. This building comprised three superposed levels, in the image of Noah's Ark as described in the Book of Genesis. On the ground floor, the Salle de l'Aquilon is the Romanesque almonry where poor pilgrims were welcomed and fed: the Rule of St. Benedict required that they be received as if they were Christ himself.

On the first floor there was a beautiful chamber, known today as the Salle du Promenoir. It had a variety of uses originally, as the difficulties of building on that terrain meant that as many functions as possible were united under one roof. In essence a refectory, it was also the chapter room, where the monks met daily to listen to readings from the Rule and to receive orders from the Father Abbot. It may also have been a scriptorium (workroom).

The upper floor was occupied by the dormitory. This panelled room, of which only a small part remains today, was at the height of the church, to which it had direct access for the service of the nocturnal offices: vigils and matins. Other elements were in annexe to it, notably the latrines, a kitchen on the first floor and infirmary next to the dormi-

Under the western terrace, a Romanesque chamber, recently unearthed, displays the remains of a superb painted scene: it shows a pattern of fleurs-de-lys (13th century), a reminder of the religious devotion of the Kings of France to the rock of the Archangel.

The arches of the cloister

The vaulting in the Cloister constitutes an important milestone in the history of architecture. The original vaulting, which was destroyed by the collapse of the north wall of the nave of the church in 1103, was replaced in about 1106. Now, by this time, some Norman craftsmen had just perfected a new method of roofing, destined for a long history: the ogival arch. This consists of a frame of stone ribs which cross through a central keystone. The Romanesque arch, which was a massive thickness in a single block, was thus able to be replaced by an articulated series of slim arches in each section. The overall weight, now considerably reduced, was supported by the ribs and concentrated on the spring points, between which the wall was no longer load-bearing. In the middle of the 12th century, some architects from the Paris area would make this innovation the starting point for Gothic architecture (the choir of the Church of Saint Denis, completed in 1144). The arches of the Cloister, still Romanesque in their heaviness, were one of the prototypes for this new system: the first ogival arches, built in the church at Lessay (Manche), date from 1098, or only 10 years earlier than those of the Cloister.

tory. On the other side of the nave, to the south, a construction made up of large archways housed an area for funerals, with a cemetery and ossuary, where the monks were buried and also some lay persons who wished to lie at the feet of the Archangel. At the start of the 12th century, Abbot Roger II (11061123) extended the monastery with the addition of a large building on the north side of the rock, now the site of the Merveille. Nothing is known about this building, which disappeared in the fire at the abbey in 1204.

Other buildings were also added by Robert de Thorigny, Abbot of the Mont from 1154 to 1186. This famous monk was one of the great figures of his time. A high-flying administrator, he was also a writer, historian, diplomat and adviser to the King of England, Henry II.

Abbot Robert had built on the south west side of the monastery a hostelry to accommodate pilgrims of a higher social standing and, above the western entrance, a group of rooms for administrative use. The abbey was in effect a seignory whose estates had to be managed and feudal rights exercised: two sinister dungeons, buried in the very depths of the western basement, are a reminder that the Abbot, though a Father to his monks, was also a Lord Justice!

Robert de Thorigny, who put the finishing touches to the Romanesque monastery, now rests beneath a humble granite slab, trodden by the feet of visitors to the terrace of the church.

ight : ***La Salle de 'Aquilon forms the round floor of the omanesque ionastery.***

he lodgings of bbot Robert de horigny 2nd half of the 2th century).

The gothic monastery

In 1204, the King of France, Phillippe-Auguste, took possession of Normandy, which had been a part of the kingdom of England since the Battle of Hastings in 1066. During this war, the Breton troops serving the French king set fire to the Mont and the abbey sustained considerable damage. Reconstruction work was begun, financed by the King and actively pursued from 1211 to 1228. This new monastery, erected in place of the ruined building of Roger II, was so beautiful, that since then it has been known as La Merveille - The Marvel!

Its overall design was highly ambitious from the outset. The plan was, in effect, to construct a group of three buildings, aligned on an east-west axis, each comprising three levels. The project would thus achieve the vertical transposition of an important figure of Christian symbolism: the square divided into 9 compartments (3x3). This geometric device, the basis for major monuments such as the tower-porch at Saint Benoît sur Loire, is the reference grid used for the design of the New Jerusalem, as described in the Book of Revelations : a square city with three doors in each side. Once again, we are reminded of the arrogance of the architectural programme!

Each of the three buildings planned was designed with a symbolic theme, as sometimes occurs with the chapters of a book. This thematic shaping, requiring a high degree of intellectual rigour, is evidence of the influence of the universities, then in the process of being established in the towns, with which Mont Saint Michel had close links.

The first building to be built, to the east, contains, moving from the bottom to the top, first the Almonry, where the poorest pilgrims were received, then the Salle des Hôtes (Guest Chamber) where the higher-ranking visitors feasted, and the monks' refectory. This superposition represents the hierarchy of medieval society, formalized in the 11th century: "those who work, those who fight and those who pray", which

_eft :
The two chambers of the first floor of La Merveille have different atmospheres : elegance and lightness in the Salle des Hôtes, and the impression of serene solidity in the Scriptorium.

would later become, in reverse order "Clergy, Nobility and Third-Estate".

The next building contained, on the ground floor, the provision storeroom, then above, the monks' workroom or scriptorium, and at the top the cloister, a place of prayer and meditation. Thus the nour-ishment of the body, the mind and the soul were superposed, the material, the intellectual and the spiritual.

The west building, finally, was to house at the lowest level, a courtroom, symbolizing justice, believed in the Middle Ages to be the most important of the four cardinal virtues; on the first floor, a new infirmary was to represent charity, the first of the three theological virtues; and on the second floor a chapter house would have signified obedience, a fundamental monastic virtue according to the Rule of St. Benedict: in this way the virtues are shown to us in the hierarchical order of Benedictine perfection.

Only two of these buildings were built. The transfer of the entrance, from the west to the east of the abbey in the middle of the 13th century, disrupted the internal organization of the monastery. So the infirmary and the courtroom were built elsewhere, but not the planned chapter room, which is evidence of the decline of the Benedictines at this period, which saw the disappearance of the mendicant orders, Franciscans and Dominicans.

Of the completed sections, there remains today the Almonry and the storeroom on the ground floor, in which the architectural simplicity is an illustration of rational functionality. The Salle des Hôtes, on the first floor, is a room fit for princely entertainment, a light and open space, achieved with a dramatic verticality. In contrast, the adjacent scriptorium has a tranquil solidity: divided in four both vertically and horizontally, it is a perfectly rationalized space, an ideal setting for intellectual work; its great circular bays, symbolic images of the celestial world, are a reminder that a monk's work is inspired by Heaven and must be dedicated to it.

On the upper floor, the refectory is a long, single nave without a bay. This dining room, in which not only the body but also the mind was to be nourished in silence by the meditation sustained by the chant of the reader officiating in the pulpit, is a contemplative space, unified by an invisible light. From the entrance, the side walls seem plain until the daylight streams through: the windows, fine lancets hidden at the back of the embrasures, become visible as one moves through the chamber; closing once again behind one. This space, closed to the world, is thus overwhelmed by light which, in medieval philosophy, was the visible sign of the divine presence in the Creation.

Below :
the Refectory, where the union of light and space brings total spirituality.

The cloister

Despite its unusual arrangement, vertical rather than horizontal, the cloister was at the centre of the organization of monastery life. The refectory and kitchen open onto the east gallery, from the south there is access to the church and the dormitory, to the west lies the charter room which housed the valuables and the records: this little building, on the north-west corner, also contains a staircase which leads directly to the scriptorium; finally the triple bay on the same side, which opens onto a void, was to link with the chapter room which was never built.

This cloister is on a human scale. The dimensions of the human body are reflected in the height and distancing of the small columns and their spacing has been set to the rhythm of a slow and meditative walk. This setting in proportion makes it an intimate place, which bears witness to the concern of the Rule to ensure the individual blossoming of the monks.

The cloister's originality lies in the staggered double row of columns arranged in quincunx. The technical role of this system has often been overestimated, in an echo of Viollet-Le-Duc. In fact, the galleries, which support neither stone vaulting nor superstructure, are light enough to pose no problems of stability. The main interest of this arrangement lies elsewhere. The two rows of slim columns spaced at half-intervals create an impression of a moving space which seems to be endlessly turning on itself. The eye is never checked by corner pieces or buttresses or even by carvings as the wall is smooth on the garden side. The cloister, through this dynamic effect, is perceived as a symbolically circular space.

In this way it evokes, following medieval tradition, the Garden of Eden, which provides the theme for the idealized foliage of the carvings. But the cloister also represents, through its square design and the richness of its materials, the New Jerusalem described in Revelations as a city of precious stones: shelly limestone, imported at great expense from England for the columns, Caen stone for the carvings and shining multi-coloured glazed tiles for the roofing (the current roof, which dates from 1965, is in this sense a mistake!). In this enclosed garden, suspended in the sky, the origins and the end of the Creation are telescoped, abolishing the passage of time and summarizing in its completeness the perfection of the Divine work, from Alpha to Omega.

The same programme, joining the beginning and the end of the world created in a cycle contained in its own perfection, can also be read in the carved decoration, which should be imagined in its original brightly painted state. This reading should be carried out following the path of the sun, which runs from morning to night and represents a summary of the history of the Universe.

On the east side, much restored around

1880, a grape-picker represents Noah, the holy wine-grower of religious history. The theologians of the Middle Ages regarded him as a prefiguration of Jesus, as in the Old Testament he is the saviour of humanity at the time of the Flood. Here he is announcing the coming of Christ, whose cross is carved on his left.

At the centre of the south gallery, a Virgin in majesty, surrounded by angels praising her, presents, as in the portal at Chartres, her child on her knees: the incarnation. To the west, towards the setting sun, Christ is dying on the Cross, then reappears in the next picture in the form of Christ risen in majesty. On the same side, the founder St. Aubert, who indicates the beginning, has been replaced further on by St. Francis of Assisi, canonized in 1228 and who indicates the present for the builders.

Finally the north, where the Lamb, which according to the Book of Revelations lights the New Jerusalem, indicates the end of time. As we are in a closed system, this same side is that of the Creation, evoked in particular by the monster devouring a bunch of grapes, symbolizing the committing of the original sin.

This book of stone, which tells the story of the Creation and the Salvation, is signed: the designer Dorn Garin engraved his name above the Virgin in the south gallery, as well as the two sculptors, Maître Roger and Maître Jean who moreover carved their self-portraits to the west, above St. Francis of Assisi.

The eastern gallery.

Details of the carvings. From top to bottom : Original sin ; Noah, a prefiguration of Christ ; the Virgin and Child, symbolising the Incarnation ; Christ crucified ; the risen Christ; the Lamb of the Resurrection in the New Jerusalem.

The garden

It is possible that there was originally a real garden in the cloister, but it must have been abandoned fairly soon afterwards due to problems of watertightness, because it no longer existed at the start of the 17th century. Restored in 1623 and planted with box and flowers, it was removed once more in 1676. The current garden, created in 1966, was designed by Father Bruno de Senneville, the founder of the current religious community. Around a central motif of box and old-fashioned Provins rose bushes, small beds of medicinal herbs enclose a lawn: the choice of plants has been carefully thought out to provide subtle harmonies of colour throughout the year.

Left : *general view.*

Photo Marc Déceneux

The flamboyant gothic choir

On 20 September 1421, while the Hundred Years' War was raging, the Romanesque choir of the church, built four hundred years earlier, collapsed. The problems of the war and of politics meant that it took twenty-five years to organize and finance its rebuilding, which did not start until 1446. The work, at first carried out briskly, slowed down and the project was not finished until 1521.

The initial impetus for the rebuilding came from Abbot Guillaume d'Estouteville (1444-1482), whose brother Louis had been the heroic Captain of the fortress during the war. This prelate was a highly important figure: a Cardinal, Archbishop of Rouen, Bishop of Ostia, he was in charge, besides the abbey of Mont Saint Michel, of those of Léhon, Cunault, Saint Gildas des Bois and soon after, Saint Ouen de Rouen. He was also a legate of Pope Nicholas V and in 1448 was even one of the leading candidates for the Throne of St. Peter. This lavish patron granted the work to one of his own master builders, whose sign is found on the beautiful church of Saint Ouen at Rouen.

The old abbey chronicles state that the Romanesque choir collapsed down to the foot of its pillars. This detail means that the 11th century crypt remained intact. It was therefore re-used and its masonry incorporated into the walls of the new crypt. This was known - with good reason - as the Crypte des Gros Piliers (Crypt of the Huge Pillars).

This sombre and austere room, quite undecorated, is crowded with enormous cylindrical pillars (six metres in circumference!) which give it a labyrinthine and oppressive character. This awesome atmosphere is in keeping with one of the functions of the crypt, which unlike the three others, is not a place of worship. It was a passage between the abbey quarters, to the south, and the cloister to the north, but above all, it was the antechamber for the courtroom, Belle-Chaise, located above the Salle des Gardes (Guardroom), the abbey entrance since the 13th century. One can well imagine the state of mind of the accused, awaiting their appearance before the court, in this nightmarish "waiting room"!

The ambience of the upper floor is quite different. Two words describe the atmosphere of the choir: simplicity and verticality. The long mouldings which cover the pillars make them extremely slender, and small,

The Flamboyant Gothic choir, a space amplified in light and height, the architectural expression of the Michaelian mystery. On the floor below, the imposing masses of the Crypte des Gros Piliers (Crypt of the Huge Pillars).

The exterior of the choir ; the flying buttresses reinforce each pillar at the point of greatest pressure from the arches.

fine columns spring with one bound from the floor to the keystones of the vaulting, a height of twenty-five metres. The eye is thus drawn to the great upper windows, without interruption from any sculptural detail. Here is, in graphic form, the same symbolic programme of a space increasing in light and height, imagined by the master builder of the 11th century as he designed a church built like a stairway. This masterpiece of aerial elegance, a veritable cage of light, is strongly supported on the outside by a battery of elegant flying- buttresses: these great arches, fine and majestic, reinforce each pillar to prevent them shifting under the weight of the vaulting. The choir of the abbey church, a faultless achievement of Gothic architecture, was, until the restorations of the 19th century, the last major building project on the Mont.

The lacework staircase

To the south east of the choir, the abutment of one flying buttress is far more massive than its neighbours. It contains a spiral staircase which leads to the terrace above the ambulatory and to the radiating chapels, then continues with an upper flight. This contains a very narrow, straight stairway of fifteen steps, known as "l'escalier de dentelle" or "lacework staircase" owing to the delicacy of its finely carved balustrade. This handrail leads to the circular walkway at the top of the choir wall, from which the eye is struck by unforgettable views of the boundless sea. This walkway, of which there are other examples (Church of La Trinité at Vendôme, the Cathedral at Metz...) may have been used as a lookout point, but was principally used as a means of access to the heights of the building by the roofers, masons and glaziers.

"A toad in a reliquary"

The great wheel

Under the monumental staircase which leads to the abbey church, the great portals of the former ossuary house the hoist, a lifting device which was installed at the beginning of the 19th century by the prison authorities to haul up supplies to the prison. It consists of a gigantic wheel, six metres in diameter, inside which the prisoners walked. Each turn of the device wound the cable round the axle and so pulled a truck up a stone rail, still visible today. It is estimated that a team of six men could haul up loads of the order of two tonnes, without too great an effort due to the high reduction ratio. This system of lifting, using the weight of manual labour as a motor, has been used for centuries. The Romans knew of it and it was used in the Middle Ages on all the great building works. Some wheels of this type, from the Medieval period, have been preserved in the great churches. The one in the Cathedral at Sées, especially, is still in use today for maintenance and restoration work.

The concordat, concluded in 1516 between Pope Leo X and King François I, was the death sentence for the Benedictine movement: the abbots were henceforth no longer elected by their monks, but appointed by the royal power, whether or not they were clergymen. This was rule by "commend".

These commendatory abbots were noblemen who collected the income from the monastery and lived elsewhere. The monks, left to themselves, rapidly sank into a dissolute life of women, hunting dogs and taverns.

To this were added the troubles of the Wars of Religion. The Protestant soldiers of the Count of Montgomery tried to take the Abbey several times: in 1577, disguised as pilgrims, they were identified and disarmed in time; another time (1591) a hundred or so of them got into the monastery through the hoist into the cellar, but betrayed by the monk who was to let them in, they were all put to death.

This period of decadence and disorder ended in 1622, when the Abbey was joined with the Congregation of St. Maur. The monks of the new persuasion were monks fired with zeal and like their predecessors in the Middle Ages, they divided their time between prayer and work. We owe to them the first historical studies of the Abbey.

The modern period is also that of the prison. Louis XI, a fervent pilgrim to Mont Saint Michel, made the monastery into a state gaol: the enemies of the kingdom were thus entrusted to the Archangel who, during the Hundred Years' War, had protected the King of France's cause. An iron cage - the famous "fillette" - was even suspended from the vaulting of one of the remotest rooms in the western substructures. Subsequently, the successors of Louis XI used this sure means of exile in the same way.

In 1793, following the departure of the last of the monks, the whole of the monastery became a prison while the rock, by a curious irony of history was rechristened

A souvenir of the prison : bolts and dungeons.

"Mont Libre" - Free Mount! The abbey, become the "Bastille of the Sea" was to be, for seventy years, one of the most important penal institutions in France. The common law prisoners mixed with the political ones, the counter-revolutionaries and the non-juring priests, then revolutionaries (Gracchus Baboeuf, Martin Bernard, Auguste Blanqui, Armand Barbès...).

The buildings were subjected to appalling alterations. Disfigured by the addition of floors and partitions, the great rooms and the nave of the church became cells, workshops and warehouses. There the prisoners made wooden clogs, felt slippers and straw hats.

During this period, when the Romantic movement brought the Middle Ages back into fashion, the intelligentsia was infuriated by the treatment inflicted on the venerable abbey. Victor Hugo, in particular, wrote on visiting this historic place: "it's like a toad in a reliquary!"...Under pressure from these influential thinkers, an imperial decree closed the prison on Mont Saint Michel. The prison went out of existence; however it was to remain a potent theme in the modern mythological image of the Mont.

The Classical facade of the abbey church (1780). The work of the Benedictines of Saint Maur, it was built following the shortening of the nave, after the fire of 1776.

Renaissance...

The closing of the prison in 1863 was very unpopular with the inhabitants of the Mont who relied on the prison for their main income. But before long, the nascent tourist industry offered the village a new source of economic development. While the Mont received, in 1860, 10,000 visitors per year, the classing of the abbey as an Historical Monument in 1874, the construction of the causeway in 1880 and the commencing of the restoration made the rock a leading tourist attraction and in 1910, 100,000 people came to explore this unique place. Today, two and a half million visitors from all over the world pass through the gateway into the village; a third of them walk up to the top to visit the abbey.

At the present time, it is the most-visited historic monument in France, after the ones in Paris. It has been the subject, since 1872, of unflagging restoration work which has over the years made it possible to regain the grandiose beauty of the monastery. The early work, carried out by Edouard Corroyer and Victor Petitgrand, gave the Mont the definitive outline we know today: the clock tower was built in 1894; the spire crowned by the statue was finished in 1898.

More than a thousand years of history, and life goes on ....

More recently, technological progress in construction techniques have enabled an extraordinary tour de force: thanks to prestressed concrete, the crypt of Notre Dame sous Terre regained its original area under the direction of Yves-Marie Froidevaux. After clearing it of the masonry which had congested it since the 11th century, the architect was able to take down the 18th century wall which masked its two small apses and supported the Clas-

The bustling scene of the main street.

The office of Vespers celebrated by the community of monks.

sical facade of the church: today this is supported by a double beam of concrete, strengthened with tensioned steel cables concealed in the thickness of the arches. This operation, executed in 1960, was an exceptional technical achievement.

At the same time as the buildings, spiritual life was also undergoing restoration. From 1867 to 1886, a first community of Brothers, from the Order of Saint Edme de Pontigny, had occupied the monastery buildings. But above all, the celebrations of the millennium of the monastery in 1966 marked the beginning of a religious revival: in 1969, a first Benedictine monk settled in the deserted abbey quarters, soon to be joined by other Brothers and Sisters. This community, which today has five members, lives in the abbey according to the Rule of St. Benedict and continues a tradition of prayer and welcome more than a thousand years old! Anyone who has experienced their hospitality will always leave a piece of his heart at Mont Saint Michel...

The famous salt-marsh sheep.

Practical information

For advice on touring or exploring the Bay of Mont Saint Michel : Maison de la Baie
50530 Genets,
Tel. : 02 33 70 86 46.

Tourist Office at Mont-Saint-Michel
Tel. : 02 33 60 14 30

The Abbey of Mont Saint Michel :
Open all year (Closed 1st January, 1st May, 1st November, 11th November, 25th December).

Guided tour (duration 1 hour) and tour with lecture (duration 2 hours),
Tel. : 02 33 60 14 14.

Monastic Community of Mont-Saint-Michel
BP 3, 50116,
Le Mont-Saint-Michel,
Tel. : 02 33 60 14 47.

Pilgrimages Office
BP 1, 50116
Le Mont-Saint-Michel.

The manuscripts from Mont Saint Michel are exhibited during the summer in the splendid Library, recently renovated and air-conditioned, of the ancient town of Avranches. They constitute one of the most beautiful collections of illuminated manuscripts from the Romanesque period in France and in Europe.
Tel. : 02 33 68 33 18.

Bibliography

Works of reference

BAZIN (Germain) : *Le Mont-Saint-Michel* (Mont Saint Michel), New York Art Books, 1978, Expanded and updated reprint of the original 1933 edition.

GOUT (Paul) *Le Mont-Saint-Michel* (Mont Saint Michel), Brussels, Culture et Civilisation, 1979. Reprint of the original 1912 edition.

MILLÉNAIRE MONASTIQUE DU MONT-SAINT-MICHEL, (The Monastic Millennium of Mont Saint Michel), Anthology.

VOLUME 1 : *Histoire et vie monastique* (Monastic Life and History), Paris, 1967.

VOLUME 2 : *Vie montoise et rayonnement intellectuel* (Life on the Mont and Intellectual Influence), Paris, 1967.

VOLUME 3 : *Culte de saint Michel et pèlerinages au Mont* (The Cult of St Michael and Pilgrimages to the Mont), Paris, 1971.

VOLUME 4 : *Sources et bibliographie générale* (Sources and General Bibliography), Paris, 1967.

VOLUME 5 : *Études archéologiques* (Archaeological Studies), Paris, 1993.

Specific monographs

DECAËNS (Henry) : *La belle époque au Mont-Saint-Michel* (La Belle Epoque on Mont Saint Michel), Editions Ouest-France, 1985.

GUILLOU (Louis-Marie), LEGENDRE (Claudine), RETERE (Christian) : *La nature en baie du Mont-Saint-Michel* (Nature in the Bay of Mont Saint Michel), Editions Ouest-France, 1985.

DOSDAT (Monique) : *L'enluminure romane au Mont-Saint-Michel* (Romanesque Illumination at Mont Saint Michel), Editions Ouest-France, 1991.

DÉCENEUX (Marc) : *Mont-Saint-Michel, histoire sacrée et symbolique* (Mont Saint Michel, Sacred and Symbolic History), Editions Ouest-France, 1993.

MAUXION (André) : *Découvrir la baie du Mont-Saint-Michel* (Exploring the Bay of Mont Saint Michel), in course of preparation.

Front cover :
General view of south side.

Front fly-leaves :
The sea, the rock, the sky : an eternal alliance.

Rear fly-leaves :
Night-time enchantment.

Title page :
North-west view.
Photo J.-M. Lebreton

On centre double page :
Illustration by Robert-Henri Martin

I.S.B.N. 2.7373.1822.X - Dépôt légal : février 1995 - N° d'éditeur : 3211.04.03.11.00
Maquette :IES - Photogravure : ERNIO - Impression et reliure : GRAFO, Bilbao, Espagne.

GW01606786

LITTLE MOLE
and His Little Car

LITTLE MOLE
and His Little Car

Concept and Illustrated by Zdeněk Miler
Written by Eduard Petiška
Translated by Mike and Tereza Baugh

Albatros

ISBN 978-80-00-02989-4

So many cars.
So many!

Just look at how many are driving here! There are green ones and red ones, blue ones and yellow ones. They're up there and down here. Not all of them can fit in the picture.
Who could ever draw all the cars driving in the city?

Now why are there islands of grass between the cars? They are there so the cars going down don't crash into the ones going up. So every car drives the right way, and everything is ok. Have a nice trip!

Now whoever was playing here in the grass? Who was scratching and digging here, and made this dirt pile? Children? A dog, perhaps? It seems to me like the dirt pile is alive. It's growing and growing, bigger and bigger.

Cars are driving by it and they don't even notice. Those cars. They are always in a hurry and never stop for dirt piles. Well, pay attention and soon we'll find out what is happening in the grass. Now here it is! Somebody is peeking out of the dirt hill. Welcome to the city, Little Mole! Take a nice look at everything around.
"Oh boy, what a nice car!" cheers Little Mole. "I bet it belongs to that dog. I didn't know that dogs even drive in cars."
No mole had ever seen such wonders. How could they? Moles live in fields and meadows, not cities.

“Oh, I wish I had a little car like that! If dogs can ride in cars, why can’t a mole? And what kind of car would I choose? Red, green, or blue? Or maybe yellow. I would only need a little tiny car—just as long as it ran. I would turn the steering wheel, the motor would hum happily, and if I were in the mood, I would honk the horn. Oh I wish I had a little car like that.”

What is going on here? Is this where they make cars? No, they're just fixing them.
Little Mole watches and mumbles: "I didn't know that cars are made from different parts. If I had those parts I would make a car in a jiffy. I can build tunnels underground and nice molehills on the grass, why couldn't I build a car?

What big wheels! I wouldn’t need wheels that big. But every car needs wheels or else it can’t drive. It seems to me that tires are actually the most important thing. But where can I get them? If I had them, I would start building a car right away.

And I shouldn’t forget about the chassis. If a car didn’t have a floor, where would the seats go? And where would I put the wheels? The wheels would fly off and I would be sitting on the road.

Now that I see a car from below, I would almost say that the chassis is the most important part of a car. The chassis and the wheels. Then you can drive. Just some pedals and a steering wheel, and you betcha, you can drive."

"What are you carrying there, Little Mole?" asks curious Little Mouse. "I bet you'd like to know, Little Mouse, but I won't tell you," says Little Mole. "Tell me, Little Mole, what you're going to build. Maybe I could offer you some advice," Little Mouse responds. "I'm going to build something that honks, hums, rattles, and goes. Something little mice don't understand," explains Little Mole.

"Nobody knows how much work goes into building a car. I've run around half the city and I'm still missing a lot. A few screws, a couple of parts and I'll be ready to get to work. I'm lucky I got this can. If only it weren't so heavy.

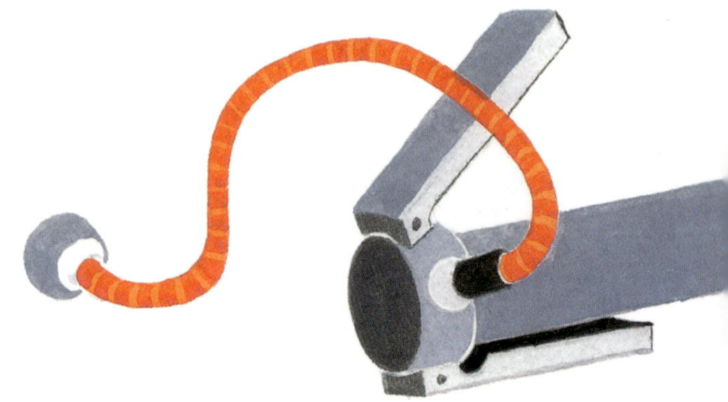

You think I won't be able to build a little car from all this? Just wait until you see what I can do!

But where to begin? Where do I start? Should I first put together the roof and floor, then attach the tires, or would it be better to put the tires together and attach the roof and floor to them, or should I start with the steering wheel? What do you think?
I've got it. I'll start from the middle. Everything lying here belonged to a car. When I put it all together, it can't be anything else but a car.

It's ready to go! Little Butterfly, do you want a ride? Take a seat on the roof and be careful that you don't fall off. What's going on? It's not working. I'm stepping on the pedals, I'm turning the wheel, but the car doesn't want to move. Are you angry with me, my little car? Why don't you want to drive? You aren't humming or even rattling, and when I want to honk, I have to shout 'toot toot.' My little car, why don't you want to drive me anywhere?

The car will not budge at all. What can I do? After all I've done, all the screws and gears and wires and parts I put together! And now my car won't listen to me.

Now what is that rolling by? Oh no! It's the wheel of a car. Or just the tire? A tire, a real tire and it's little! If I could find three more, that would be something. My car would finally work.

One, two, three, four tires.
Who could have sent them to me?
They were rolling over the grass, I just barely caught them. Hey, what's that racket? Someone is hammering over there. I'll put one tire around my neck like a little collar, the second on my head like a little hat, and the third and fourth I'll carry in my paws.

And now I'll go
see what's going
on over there."

Oh no, what a mess! A minute ago it was a beautiful little car. When the key was turned, it drove and rumbled almost like a big car that carries people. But Charlie took a hammer and pounded on it until it was just some tin and gears. And why did he do it? Because he likes breaking toys. Doesn't he know that he shouldn't do that?

Of course he knows.
That's why he's
running away.

"Such a beautiful little car,
it would be perfect for me.
It would drive, have real wheels,
seats, and a steering wheel.
It did drive, but now it can't.
It's smashed up and crumpled.
It's a sick little car, a really sick
little car. If only I knew of
someone who could make it
better again."

“What’s wrong, Little Mole?” asks curious Little Mouse.
“My dear mouse, I built a car and it didn’t go so well. It won’t drive. And now I found a beautiful little car, but it’s completely wrecked and I can’t fix it. It’s a shame that you can’t fix cars.”
“No, I really can’t,” said Little Mouse, “but I do know where to go for help.” And she pointed at a house across the street.

"I was afraid that I wouldn't be able to carry everything. It's a good thing that I don't have too far to go. Ouch, these tires are too heavy. And I'm so hot! Lucky you, you don't have to wear a fur-coat in the summer like me

Oh shoot, did I lose the key? I didn’t. Oh good.
Without the key I couldn’t wind up the car.

AUTO SE

Just tell me what magic they do here? Is it really real? Can they really make a broken car new again? Well, Little Mouse must know what goes on in the city. She's been through every nook and cranny. I'll try and see.

Wow, this is neat. Look at that. A crane like that could lift me right up too. Up, up, and away. Just come back to me someday.
I'll wait here so you can find me.

What a beauty! That's so nice of you, Mr. Crane, that you brought me my little car. And will it really drive? Can I really sit in it and turn the steering wheel? And honk the horn? I'll be really careful with it—I'll drive safely, so I don't break it."

First I'll put the key in and wind up the car. Vroom, vroom—how nicely it growls. Once, twice, three times…slowly, slowly so the spring doesn't break. Hold on, my precious little car. We'll go for a drive and then I'll show you where I live. Look, little car, that's my mouse friend who gave me such good advice. Little Mouse, would you like to go for a ride?"

"No thank you, Little Mole. What if the neighbor's black cat saw us. Go by yourself, just make sure you don't run over anyone!"

"Uh oh, what's happening? My car just stopped. Toot, toot, the other cars honk. They want to go. All the cars are in a rush. The first car is going on a trip, the second is taking a little girl to her grandma, the third is carrying lemonade, the fourth is carrying apples and pears, and the fifth and sixth are carrying… who can remember it all.

And my little car is standing in their way.

—Oh right, little car, I forgot that I need to wind you up. I'll wind you up right away."
Toot, toot, the other cars honk.
"Stop honking, I'm going now, I won't be in the way. See, you can't drive without gas and I have to wind my car up. Vroom, vroom—what a beautiful sound! My precious little car, you vroom better than all the other cars in the world.

I barely stopped in time. I almost ran over an ant. Little ant, this isn't the right place to cross the street, what if someone hit you! First, look left, and then right, and then you can cross the street. These days every little boy knows that.
Look at me, doggy. Did you think that cars are only for people and dogs? Now you're sitting in a car that is stopped. But mine is going—if you weren't so big, I'd give you a ride. But you're really big and you'd break my car."

Just look at how many cars are driving here! There are green ones and red ones, blue ones and yellow ones. Not all of them can fit in the picture. Where are the cars going? It's evening and the cars are shining their lights so they don't get lost. And who is driving in that little car? Little Mole, and he is also shining his lights to find his way home.

"We're home, little car.
Here is where I live, and
you'll live here with me.
Sweet dreams, little car.
I'm going to sleep.
I'll take the key with me so
nobody drives off with you
in the night.
What do you think of my
car, bluebells? Do you like it
too? Make sure you wake
me up early so I don't sleep
in. Good night, little car."

Zdeněk Miler – Eduard Petiška

Little Mole
and His Little Car

Illustrated and concept by Zdeněk Miler
Written by Eduard Petiška
Translated from the Czech by Mike and Tereza Baugh
Graphic Design by Milada Čvančarová
Cover design by Soňa Šedivá
Editor Šárka Krejčová
Production Petra Mejstříková
Published in Prague in 2012 by Albatros
Albatros is an imprint of Albatros Media a. s.
Na Pankráci 30, Praha 4, Czech Republic
Printed and bound in Tiskárny Havlíčkův Brod, a. s., Husova 1881, HB, 2018
4th English Edition

www.albatros.cz
www.albatrosmedia.cz

The price indicated by the manufacturer is a recommended retail price.